Milk Carton

Leonardo Reynoso Lizarraga

India | USA | UK

Presentation by *BookLeaf Publishing*

Web: www.bookleafpub.com

E-mail: info@bookleafpub.com

ISBN: 9789360944223

First edition 2024

To the boy on the milk carton who looks too much like me.

ACKNOWLEDGEMENT

I would like to thank my friends, the ones who stayed and listened to me ramble relentlessly about my poetry for months on end in preparation for this collection. Your patience was not lost on me.

I would also like to thank my mother and father for encouraging my writing and never doubting my ability to get published for a second.

PREFACE

The title of "Milk Carton" was chosen to encapsulate the idea of feeling lost as a movement to find missing kids was given around 1984 in the United States. This movement included placing photos of the missing children with the question "Have you seen me?" typed underneath it. After the creation of the Amber Alert system, the usage of the milk carton pictures has died out almost completely. These poems are not to make light of the tragic reality of the milk cartons. The symbolism of the milk carton pictures is used as a method of self-discovery and inner-child healing in a modern society that has forced so many children to grow up.

Lamoureux, A. (2020, September 9). The real reason they stopped putting missing kids on milk cartons. Grunge.com. https://www.grunge.com/243257/the-real-reason-they-stopped-putting-missing-kids-on-milk-cartons/

Milk Carton

The milk has gone sour.
The carton no longer fits it.

It's always a morning ritual
with myself.

I'll leave half of me in bed.
Let the tired and steady me
pour out a new bowl
of dry cereal.

As I eat,
the picture on the carton
looks familiar,
like the kid that I was supposed
to grow up to be.

A young boy:
Carefree and curious.
"Have you seen me?"

As I wash the plates,
I'll look at the sleepy sunrise.
I'll find the energy
to wake the better half of me.

Maybe today I'll find him.
Maybe today
I'll see him in our favorite flowers
or in yellow butterfly wings,
or in the puddles of fresh rain.

I'll nestle within my other self.
holding the hands of the fearful,
anxious child
who avoids his reflection.

I'll catch his figure in our car window.
See his smile as I see it reflect myself.
All this to love the boy
on the milk carton.

Mimicry

How terrible of me
to believe that I was a hornet's nest.

Cruel to believe that shaking me meant death.
For it meant pain to be near me,

When I've made myself a
bumble bee.

Soft and full of pollen,
to spread to
all of my favorite flowers.

You caged me and broke my wings,
and in my anger, I stung.

I hurt myself in hurting you,
and though you know better,
I thought worse.

Oh, how terrible of me to forget
how to be sharp is to be soft.

Work In Progress

"Who will love you,
If you cannot love yourself?"

I will.
I will look at you as
The unfinished artwork that you are,
And sit patiently until you finish.

Only if you let me…
Only if you don't let the
Empty of the canvas get to you.
Only if you take care of yourself.

I'll bring you water on
the days you work so busily
That your body
Becomes a second thought–

Only if you promise to drink it.
Only if you realize why I do it,
Only if you know it too.

I'll sit at my own easel, and work.
Remind myself that the empty white
Is not absence
But the possibility of everything.

And when you bring me a glass,
I'll remember that dryness of my throat
And aching of my growing body.

I'll look at your canvas for inspiration,
The aloe and simple clovers,
Like ointment in my bleeding heart.
I'll paint the remedy for us.

Let me make you a home in my art.
Let me show you the conditions
To unconditional love.

Young Fire

I ache for the burn of 16.

When I knew the world
By what was given.
When the complicated seemed
Simple.

I knew who I was,
Even when I was wrong.

I ache to be angry.

To be the teen who
Demanded change.
Who felt the world was carried
On their weighted shoulders.

Forcing him to look down.
Finding sunlight in muddy puddles.

I ache for the heartbreak of 20.

Knowing I am better now.
Forgetting I was worse before.
I have so much road
Still to cover.

But I've memorized the names
Of flowers and their meanings.

I have learned my way around
Their needles and thorns,
With the scars on my hands
As reminders.

My knees ache from 16, but
My heart burns for the warmth of
Growing old.

No-One's Fault

How do I get rid
Of the weight inside my heart
That formed
When my mother no longer
Had the strength
To carry me?

Growing up

I cannot escape
The heartache of twenty.

The wish, growing into a need,
To be stuck in a frozen time-slot:
A picture of a younger me and
My dog.

To stop seeing the beautiful gray
Of my mother's hair,
Lest more of the child in my heart
Dies.

To stop the tears that keep falling
Despite my weary demands
As I see my father's love of us,
Like a golden locket, online.
Infrequent now,
But still holding the breath,
Of when my siblings and I would
Fight over silly things.
Posts of my mother and father,
Where no doubt can live,
Living as proof of their love.

I feel smaller each day,
In this body of an adult.
A loose shirt,
That I'm scared I'll grow into.

I weep,
Until the heartache of my twenties is gone.

Life is

Cyclical.
My pattern is cyclical.

I grow warm in summer sun,
Bloom and ripen,
Soak up the golden light,
And fruit into sweet peaches.

Pity that the sun
Turns my sugar against me.
My love becomes a drug
You long to drink.

In the dark, I feel myself as fluid.
Questioning, if I'm only filling
The mold of the me
I suppose I am.

Like night, I'll fall and no one will see
Myself gorging fermented flesh.
Forgetting the pit at its center:
A solidified stone of wasted potential.

Choke,
As hands dig

Trenches into my throat.
Prime land to take root.

The pit inside me hates the
Dark,
So he will tunnel out
To reach an ounce of light.

Like dawn, my jaw breaks
And the potential all unfurls.
I think I'm myself again.
I think I see the sun.

I'll bloom in the warmth.
Soak up the summer breeze.
Grow into my shape again.
Fruit into who I want to be.

I'll know it, I'll see it,
The pattern will return…

Baptism

My hands smell
Of fresh soil.
My nail beds stained copper.
Once I reach the river,
I know I'll wash it off.

The sleeping stone above my head,
Holds a name I thought I lost.

The mushrooms tucking me in In mycelium ate
me and gave me A second life.

I pulled away from the grassroots,
Cut my lifeline from the earth,
And took a new breath.
I cried and cried to fill my lungs again.

My legs gave out, once or twice,
Before I learned again what my last body
Knew so well.

Each step brings fairy lilies.
Each step brings me closer to
Salvation.

When I finally reach the river
I let myself crumble
And drink– drink until my mind
Could hold no more.

But the smell of copper stayed,
Like a "friend", on my hands:
One who knew me before I reformed.
The dirt is gone, but there's a stain.

So, I'll keep walking.
I'll learn of my old graves, and
Talk to the trees who wept at my
Burial. Who cried
As they grew from gnawed bones.

I'll keep reaching rivers,
And wash away the copper
Until I feel clean,
Or until I forget
What was me in the first place.

New Eden

You sowed roses into my chest.
I worked daily to watch them flower.

The smell was sweet and almost
Sickly.
I wore them like a pin,
A badge of honor,
With dense pride.

But when you let them wither,
You forgot to warn me of thorns.
I failed to prepare my hands, now
Decorated with tan sticky ribbons.

I chopped up the stems.
I left nothing visible.
Removed each thorn,
Until my heart could breathe again.

When the beargrass nestled in
My own fallacies showed.
The ground was too packed
From my half-hazard gardening.

Past roots laid under my chest,
Tangled and stubborn,
And if I tugged too roughly
I'd surely perish.

So bit by bit
I'm freeing myself from your claws.
Composting roots, loosing soil,
controlling fire, and growing again.

Phases

I strive to be fluid
And soft.

For my body to bounce back
As quickly as I got hit, as if
Nothing had ever hurt me.

Like a fresh rose
That keeps its flavor and softness
As it's pressed,
Dried,
Cooked,
Torn,
Or strained

Until it no longer looks like an
Untouched flower.

But when you take a deep breath
The aroma of who it has always been
Kisses your nose.

I strive to be different,
Yet undeniably a ghost
Of every form I once was.

Process

Hearts enveloped in iron bars,
Outgrown their cages
Aching with each
Thumping beat.

With each thud
The iron creaks
And the dams weaken.
Tears will flow soon.

Water cleans.
Your past is dirty.
Brace yourself
To be renewed.

Slowly break your cage,
And free your swollen heart.
Take comfort in how the river
Will calm soon.

The Aftermath of Grief:

19

I know it, and cannot explain it. Some part of me
is weeping.

Shift

With the ease of breath,
The Moon will care for you.

"You will be broken,
You will be changed,
You will make mistakes,
And you will hurt.

But had my course not been
changed by the universe's hand,
I would not have had
The honor of loving you."

Grief

I hope you find happiness. I hope it is as kind as you remember. I hope you grow old. I hope you find out whom you grow old with. I hope they love you as you love them. I hope they help build a home you want to return to. I hope you return to it each night. I hope you see your favorite flowers on your kitchen table. I hope you press the petals within these pages.

Chance

I hope we meet
In every universe:
Alive and well.

For I know that in some
I was a simple name
In the paper, that you
Cannot remember.

I was a carving in a stone
Above a pile of turned dirt
That held fresh flowers
And no heart to hold you back.

I was a photo in a frame,
Collecting dust,
Never replaced
By a newer version.

I was an idea,
A memory,
A story
Told to you.

In these universes,
You met me.

In most universes,
I hope I met you too.

Healing

When my psyche breaks,
I set it back in
Like a broken bone

And it'll mend together
Differently
Each time.

Continuity

When you were so scared of losing
Yourself,
Of not being true to yourself,
Let me assure you:

You were you last morning
And
You were you this night.

You were you when the morning sun
Blinded your eyes, as it peaks its
Lazy head.
You were you when it was so cloudy that
Your weary eyes thought they closed early.

You were you when you were born
Screaming and crying for
New breath.
You will be you when you are laid down
In a soft bed of ash and mulch.

You are you when they call you "she."
You are you when they call you "he".
You are you when they call you "they,"
Or any way your mind knows your body.

You are you when they call you
Names that bed themselves like
Hooks in your soft heart.
You are you when you find your
Name, a shiny pebble
Calling to be collected.

You were you when you felt broken,
Cutting the palms on glass shards
That were never meant to be picked up.
You forced them onto you,
Sliced away at your skin.

You will be you when you fail.
You will be you when you succeed.

You were you when you felt lost
Hibernating within yourself.
You were you when you roamed the
Mountains of "what ifs" and
Trenches of "who's that" and the
Emptiness of "why am I".
You are you when you find yourself.

You are you when you find out how to love.
You are you when you still don't know.

You are you when you look in the mirror.

27

When you are confused about who you see

That's okay.
I am here for you,
As you were, and will always be, here for you.

Me, I

Two.

Two hearts
trapped within
Two parts.

Two sides
at love and war within
two hands.

Too much
has been held within
too little.

To break apart
a single person
to fix it from within.

One turns to Two.
Two, a part of One.

The Blending of Us

Meet me
Where our rooms end.

The doorframes shall be our seats:
Thrones in which I may get to hear

Stories fill the air
In symphonies and trials.

I'll listen with three ears, to hear:
Why, what, and who you'll get to
Love
late in our life.

I'll add together my peppered thoughts,
To add warmth to friends and stone soup. I'll
bring
The bowls, if you bring the spoons.

Meet me
Where I end
And you begin,
Let the borders blend.

A Garden in the Graveyard

There is a body buried within me:

A heart within my heart.
The bones have been bleached now,
Mind is falling apart.

I've given her a garden,
For which she has become.
Her vines replace my nerves:
My spinal cord undone.

I'm more plant than flesh now.
In oak, jasmine, and rot.
I look so much happier
Than a corpse, like I, aught.

But I am not that girl.
Though she is a part of me
I live in her skin and in her honor
I dance on buried dragon teeth.

Project

I find myself in soup.
In its warmth and its weight,
I find my wet heart.

I find myself in the dirt.
Dig my bones up from the murky and muddy,
from where the growth returns.

I find myself in flowers,
The wilting of their petals adorn my soul,
And beg him to stay.

I pick up the pieces
And sew them with unsteady hands.

I pick myself up
And I'll find myself again.

www.ingramcontent.com/pod-product-compliance
Lightning Source LLC
Chambersburg PA
CBHW071236140726
47996CB00007B/2630